MINNESOTA

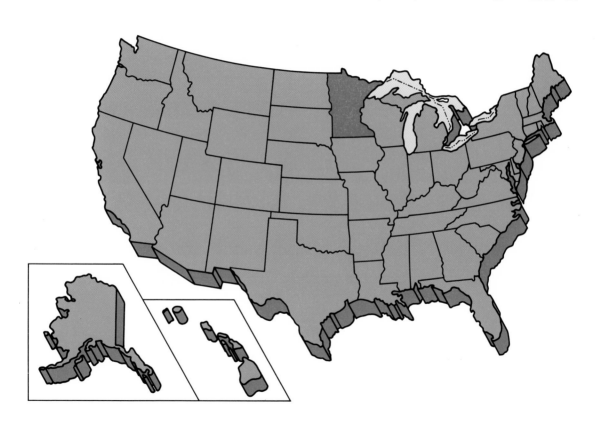

MINNESOTA

A. P. Porter

Lerner Publications Company

This book is available in two editions:
Library binding by Lerner Publications Company
Soft cover by First Avenue Editions
241 First Avenue North
Minneapolis, MN 55401
ISBN: 0–8225–2718–9 (lib. bdg.)
ISBN: 0–8225–9735–7 (pbk.)

LIBRARY OF CONGRESS
CATALOGING-IN-PUBLICATION DATA
Porter, A. P.
    Minnesota / A. P. Porter.
        p.   cm. — (Hello USA)
    Includes index.
    Summary: Introduces the geography, history,
industries, people, and other highlights of
Minnesota.
    ISBN 0–8225–2718–9 (lib. bdg.)
    1. Minnesota—Juvenile literature.
[1. Minnesota.] I. Title. II. Series.
F606.3.P67   1992
977.6—dc20   91–20622

Manufactured in the United States of America
2 3 4 5 6 7 – JR – 01 00 99 98 97 96

Cover photograph by
Patricia Drentea, *Spoonbridge
and Cherry* 1985–1988,
Claes Oldenburg and
Coosje van Bruggen
Collection Walker Art Center,
Minneapolis. Gift of
Frederick R. Weisman in
honor of his parents, William
and Mary Weisman, 1988.

The glossary that begins on
page 68 gives definitions of
words shown in **bold type** in
the text.

 This book is printed
on acid-free, recycla-
ble paper.

CONTENTS

PAGE   CHAPTER

6   Did You Know . . . ?

9   A Trip Around the State

19   Minnesota's Story

43   Living and Working in Minnesota

57   Protecting the Environment

SPECIAL SECTIONS

40   *Historical Timeline*

62   *Minnesota's Famous People*

66   *Facts-at-a-Glance*

68   *Pronunciation Guide, Glossary*

70   *Index*

Did You Know . . . ?

☐ During the winter, the town of International Falls in northern Minnesota often records the coldest daily temperature in the continental United States.

☐ Every year, anglers catch more than 500,000 pounds (227,000 kilograms) of walleye in Mille Lacs Lake in central Minnesota.

In-line skates were developed in Minnesota by Scott Olson, a former hockey player who wanted to be able to practice skating year-round.

National Smoke-Free Day, held each year on November 15, was started in the town of Monticello, Minnesota.

Waterskiing was invented on Lake Pepin in southeastern Minnesota in 1922.

During the 1930s, Saint Paul, Minnesota, was a hideout for many gangsters, including John Dillinger and George "Baby Face" Nelson.

A Trip Around the State

Minnesota, nicknamed the Star of the North, lies in the heart of North America. The second largest state in the Midwest, Minnesota is bordered on the east by Wisconsin and on the west by North and South Dakota. Canada is to Minnesota's north and Iowa is to its south. The waters of Lake Superior, one of the five **Great Lakes,** lap against Minnesota's northeastern boundary.

Glaciers covered much of Minnesota about 10,000 years ago, during the last **Ice Age.** By the time these slowly moving masses of ice and packed snow had melted, they had flattened much of Minnesota's land.

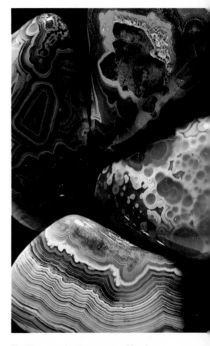

Patterned stones called agates are found in many Minnesota lakes.

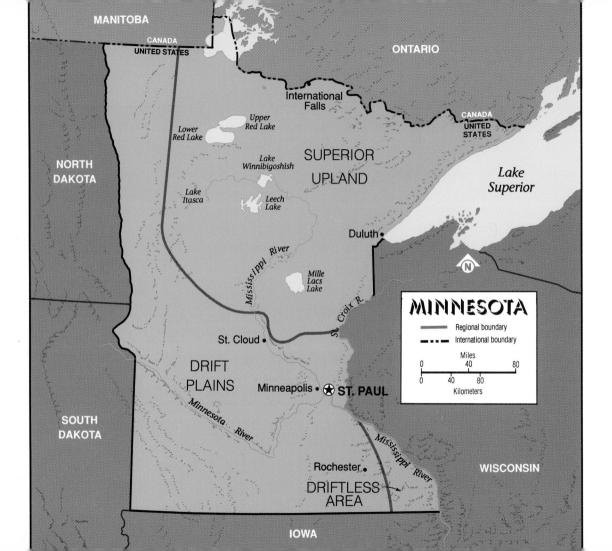

The glaciers left Minnesota with three geographic regions. They are the Superior Upland, the Drift Plains, and the Driftless Area.

The Superior Upland covers much of the northern half of Minnesota. The region is rugged and dotted with boulders. As the glaciers scraped across Minnesota, they gouged holes that later filled with water. In the northeastern corner of the state, these glacial lakes are now called the Boundary Waters because they form the boundary between Minnesota and Canada.

Lake Superior, the largest body of fresh water in the world, washes against the Superior Upland's eastern edge.

Weathered bluffs tower over rivers in southeastern Minnesota.

The Drift Plains, which lie south and west of the Superior Upland, cover almost half of Minnesota. Glaciers ground down the land in this region and left **drift**, or rich topsoil, as they melted.

The Driftless Area is in the southeastern corner of Minnesota. The region is driftless because glaciers never reached the area to flatten it and deposit drift. Instead, steep **bluffs** overlook deep river valleys.

12

Glaciers formed thousands of lakes within Minnesota, the largest of which include Upper and Lower Red Lake, Lake Winnibigoshish, Leech Lake, and Mille Lacs Lake. The Mississippi River, the longest river in the United States, begins at Lake Itasca in northern Minnesota. Most of the state's major rivers—including the Minnesota and the Saint Croix—flow into the mighty Mississippi.

Minnesotans find natural beauty and fun at the state's many lakes.

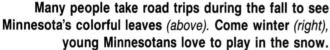
Many people take road trips during the fall to see Minnesota's colorful leaves *(above)*. **Come winter** *(right)*, **young Minnesotans love to play in the snow.**

Minnesota is famous for its cold winters, but the state has four seasons and a wide range of temperatures. In July, average temperatures are 68° F (20° C) in the north and 74° F (23° C) in the south. In January, average temperatures are 2° F (–17° C) in the north and 15° F (–9° C) in the south.

Snowstorms and bone-chilling winds are common throughout the state during the winter. An average of 70 inches (178 centimeters) of snow falls in northeastern Minnesota every year. Eastern Minnesota receives the most rain and snow in the state. The climate gets drier toward the west.

More than one-third of Minnesota is forested, mostly in the north, where pine, spruce, balsam fir, aspen, and white birch trees grow. In the pine forests, honeysuckle, wintergreen, trailing arbutus, and blueberries thrive in sunny spots. Maple, black walnut, oak, and other hardwood trees fill woodlands in the south.

Pine and birch trees grow in northern Minnesota.

15

Timber wolf

Much of Minnesota was once covered with **prairie**. This grassland had grass so tall that early explorers had to stand on the backs of their horses to see over it. Most of the prairie has been plowed to raise wheat, corn, and other crops, but prairie wildflowers such as blazing stars and asters still flourish.

Unlike many other states, Minnesota is home to several kinds of large wild animals. Most of Minnesota's wildlife lives in the northern part of the state, where people are much more scarce. Moose and black bears, along with otters, snapping turtles, bald eagles, and even timber wolves, live in the swamps and woods of the north.

White-tailed deer, mink, and beavers live throughout Minnesota. Red foxes can sometimes be found even in the state's large cities.

Minnesota's thousands of lakes are havens for ducks and geese. Mallard ducks flock to Minnesota's **wetlands.** Anglers cast their hooks for bass, walleye, northern pike, trout, catfish, and muskellunge.

Blazing star

Great blue heron

Long ago, some Native Americans lived near the swamps and lakes of what is now northern and central Minnesota. In the summer, they harvested the wild rice that grew in shallow waters—a tradition that is still practiced.

Minnesota's Story

The first people to come to the region now known as Minnesota probably arrived about 10,000 years ago. They were big-game hunters from northeastern Asia who tracked their food supply—giant bison and mammoths—across a land bridge that once connected Asia and North America. A few spear points chipped from rock are almost all that remain of these ancient people.

When the big-game hunters came, the climate was getting warmer and the glaciers were melting. As the temperature became more bearable, the lives of these early North Americans became easier. The descendants of the first people, now called Native Americans or Indians, began picking fruit and nuts and hunting squirrels, rabbits, and other small animals.

In the winter, Indian people hunted on snowshoes, which allowed them to move quickly over deep snow.

About 500 years ago, an Indian people called the Dakota, which means "friend," lived where the prairies of the Drift Plains meet the forests of the Superior Upland. In the summer, the Dakota lived in houses made of bark and wooden poles. They hunted elk, deer, and buffalo, drying part of the meat supply for winter. Then they lived in tepees made of hides.

In the 1650s, French explorers

Pierre Esprit Radisson and Médard Chouart des Groseilliers traveled to the northwestern shore of Lake Superior. They were probably the first white people in the region.

In 1680 Louis Hennepin, a **missionary** from Belgium, became the first European known to visit the site that is now the city of Minneapolis. More explorers and traders followed. Some were looking for a water route to the Pacific Ocean. Most came to make money.

The Indians traded furs to the French for items such as cloth, needles, thread, guns, and iron kettles. The French sold the furs at a great profit in Europe and Asia, where fur hats were popular.

Louis Hennepin was captured by Indians while exploring what is now Minnesota. The Indians led their captive past a waterfall on the Mississippi River. Hennepin named it the Falls of Saint Anthony.

21

In the late 1600s, Native Americans called Ojibway (or Chippewa) were moving into the northern and eastern lands of the Dakota people. The Ojibway were being pushed westward by the Iroquois Indians, who had been pushed westward by European settlers from North America's eastern coast.

The Dakota agreed to let the Ojibway stay and hunt. In return, the Dakota wanted the Ojibway to let French traders from the Great Lakes pass through Ojibway country to trade with the Dakota. The Ojibway agreed.

The pelts of otters, muskrat, and especially beavers were the furs

The thick pelts of otters made French fur traders rich.

most valued by the French. These animals grew their thickest fur in the cold north, where the Ojibway had settled. The Dakota (called Sioux by the French) wanted to live again where they could trap the best furs for trade.

Fur traders traveled by water through northern Minnesota.
When the traders reached land, they carried their canoes
and supplies to the next river or lake.

The Ojibway and Dakota started fighting each other in 1736. Gradually, the Ojibway pushed the Dakota to the south and west. By 1800 the Ojibway controlled all of what is now northern Minnesota. The Dakota still held the south, though, and the place they called *Mdo-te,* later "Mendota," became a trading center for furs and other goods.

Traders gathered at posts where they could exchange their furs for money, food, or other goods.

In 1803 France sold a huge area of land in central North America to the United States. This deal, called the Louisiana Purchase, included most of Minnesota. The Louisiana Purchase doubled the size of the United States. But the Indians living in the area knew nothing of this and believed that they were free to live and hunt there.

The large forests that covered Minnesota in the early 1800s provided the lumber used to construct many of the state's early buildings.

In 1805 explorer and U.S. Army officer Zebulon Pike was sent to Mendota, at the junction of the Mississippi and Minnesota rivers. Representing the U.S. government, Pike traded with the Dakota for land on which to build a fort. Fort Snelling, built there in 1820, was the first government outpost in the region.

Soldiers stationed at Fort Snelling built a sawmill upstream at the Falls of Saint Anthony. The soldiers cut down trees, using them as firewood and as lumber for fences and buildings. The army planted wheat and built a mill to grind the grain into flour.

By the time the fort was completed in 1824, buffalo and other animals the Indians hunted had become scarce in the area.

With their source of food gone, the Dakota and Ojibway sold their lands east of the Mississippi River to the U.S. government in 1837. Americans and Europeans began to settle on the former Indian lands. They founded the towns of Stillwater, Saint Anthony (which later became Minneapolis), and Saint Paul.

Fort Snelling housed Minnesota's first hospital and first school.

Saint Paul was a busy port by the mid-1800s. The city became the capital of the Minnesota Territory in 1849.

Lumber companies came to the Saint Croix River valley, where trees were abundant. Saint Paul, on the Mississippi River, became a major fur market.

Trappers brought furs to Saint Paul from all over the region. Some pelts arrived from the north in carts pulled by oxen or ponies. The clumsy carts took up to two months to get to Saint Paul. Steam-powered paddle wheelers carried pelts and lumber from Saint Paul and brought back paper, cloth, furniture, livestock, and food—supplies needed by the settlers.

Dakota leaders met with U.S. government officials in 1851 to sign treaties. The government paid the Indians only pennies for each acre of land it bought.

In 1851 Dakota leaders signed **treaties** selling most of southern Minnesota to the United States. Unable to read and write English, the Indian leaders also signed away some of the money they were to receive under the treaty of 1837. The Ojibway signed over almost all of the northern half of Minnesota in the treaties of 1854 and 1855.

About 8,000 Dakota were moved to a narrow strip of land along the Minnesota River. Most of the Ojibway agreed to live on small **reservations,** areas of land set aside for them, in northern Minnesota.

Immigrants (newcomers) from Germany, Ireland, Sweden, and Norway swarmed into the Minnesota Territory. Settlers soon vastly outnumbered the fewer than 20,000 Native Americans left in the area. In 1855 Minnesota had 40,000 white people. By 1857 it had 150,000. And by 1858 Minnesota had enough people to become the 32nd state in the Union.

For years, Northern and Southern states in the Union had been disagreeing over many issues, including whether Southerners should own slaves. To make sure slavery would still be legal, the Southern states decided to leave the Union. In 1861 they formed their own country, called the Confederate States of America. When Confederate troops attacked a Northern fort, the Civil War began. Minnesota was the first state to offer troops to the Union.

U.S.-Dakota Conflict of 1862

During the summer of 1862, the Dakota Indians were living on a narrow strip of land along the Minnesota River. Wildlife had been scarce, last year's crop had been ruined by cutworms, this year's crop was not ready, and the traders would not give the Indians food and goods. The government was late with their annual payment for the land they had bought from the Dakota. Without that money, the Indians could not buy food. It seemed as though the Dakota had sold their homeland for nothing.

The Dakota were starving to death. Settlers who lived nearby refused to give them food. The whites assumed that the Indians would be taken care of by the government or else thought that it was their own fault if they were suffering. Some Indians, hoping to take back their land, persuaded a Dakota chief named Little Crow to lead them in a war against the white settlers.

Little Crow expected the Dakota to lose the war, and in only a few weeks they did. Nearly 600 people, counting white settlers, soldiers, and Indians, were killed in the fighting. Thirty-eight Dakota who were charged with murder were hanged in Mankato after the war. Hundreds more Dakota were sent to prison or were forced to leave their homes in Minnesota and resettle on barren land in South Dakota. Little Crow fled Minnesota during the war but was killed when he returned in 1863.

More than 100 years later, the state of Minnesota and the Dakota people declared 1987 the Year of Reconciliation. The state recognized that both the settlers and the Dakotas had true complaints in the conflict. At a ceremony in Mankato honoring the 38 American Indians that were hanged, eagles —like spirits—were seen flying overhead.

After the Civil War, some former slaves headed north to live in states that had supported the Union. Some black men joined the U.S. Army. These soldiers were stationed at Fort Snelling.

The Civil War ended with a Union victory in 1865. Minnesota turned to building railroads and flour mills. Trains hauled Minnesota's flour, lumber, and farm goods to the East Coast. Minnesota got one of its nicknames, the Gopher State, from a newspaper cartoon that pictured gophers pulling a train across gopher-filled prairies.

In the 1860s, the U.S. government passed the Homestead Act. This law promised free land in Minnesota and other western territories to almost anyone willing to farm it. Minnesotans advertised abroad for people to make Minnesota their home. Norwegians, Swedes, Germans, and Finns came to plow up the land that had once belonged to the Dakota people.

Newspaper advertisements offering jobs and land drew new settlers to Minnesota.

3000 **LABORERS**

WANTED

On the *LAKE SUPERIOR AND MISSISSIPPI RAILROAD from Duluth at the Western Extremity of Lake Superior, to ST PAUL*

Constant Employment will be given. Wages range from \$2.00 to \$4.00 per Day.

MECHANICS
Are Needed at Duluth!

Wages to Masons and Plasterers, \$4.00 per day; Carpenters, \$3.00 per day.

10,000 **EMIGRANTS**

WANTED TO SETTLE ON THE LANDS OF THE COMPANY, NOW OFFERED ON LIBERAL CREDITS AND AT LOW PRICES.

Large bodies of Government Lands, subject to *Homestead* Settlement, or open to *Pre-Emption.* These Lands offer Facilities to Settlers not surpassed, if equalled by any lands in the West. They lie *right along the line* of the Railroad connecting Lake Superior with the Mississippi River, one of the most important Roads in the West. Forty miles of the Road are now in running order, and the whole Road (150 miles) will be completed by June, 1870. WHITE and YELLOW PINE, and VALUABLE HARDWOOD, convenient to Market, abound.

The SOIL is admirably adapted to the raising of WINTER WHEAT and TAME GRASSES. *Stock have Good Pasture until the Depth of Winter.*

The waters of Lake Superior, in connection with the Timber, make this much the warmest part of Minnesota. The navigation season at Duluth is several weeks longer than on the Mississippi. The LUMBER interest will furnish abundant and profitable *WINTER WORK.*

FREE TRANSPORTATION over the completed portion of the Railroad will be given to Laborers and all Settling on the Lands of the Company.

At Duluth *Emigrants* and their families will find *free* quarters in a new and commodious *Emigrant House,* until they locate themselves, by applying at Duluth to LUKE MARVIN, Agent. *Laborers* will report to WM. BRANCH, Contractor of the Road. For information as to Steamers to Duluth, inquire at Transportation Office in any of the Lake Cities.

DULUTH, MINN., JUNE 14, 1869.

"DULUTH MINNESOTIAN" PRINT.

Churning butter was one of many household jobs performed by Minnesota's pioneer women.

Farming was hard work. Families plowed the land, then planted and harvested crops. They repaired tools and buildings and tended the animals. The women usually sewed and mended clothes, canned and cooked food, looked after the children, and made candles and soap.

Sometimes unexpected hardships burdened families. Between 1873 and 1877, billions of grasshoppers ate up most of the crops in southwestern Minnesota. Many farmers gave up and left their farms. Others sent family members to work in logging camps or on farms untouched by the insects.

Huge swarms of grasshoppers invaded Minnesota in the late 1800s. Farmers sometimes used nets to nab the insects.

Even after the grasshoppers left, the high cost of shipping crops by railroad kept farm profits low. Farmers banded together to learn better ways to raise crops and animals. They also worked to get laws passed that would help farmers in need.

By the 1880s, Saint Paul had become a major railroad hub for the Upper Midwest. Trains from as far away as the Pacific Coast made stops at the Saint Paul depot. From southern and western Minnesota and from North and South Dakota, trains brought wheat to Minneapolis to be ground into flour at the city's flour mills.

Iron ore was first mined in northeastern Minnesota in 1884. The ore was shipped by rail to Duluth. There, it was loaded onto ships to cross Lake Superior to the steel mills that lined the Great Lakes.

Trains carried logs from lumber camps to sawmills.

TALL TALES

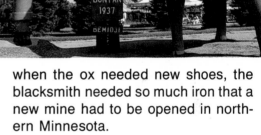

One of the best-known heroes of American folklore is the towering lumberjack known as Paul Bunyan. Many stories about Paul Bunyan and his giant blue ox, Babe, take place in Minnesota.

Babe was a big help around Minnesota's logging camps. He could haul a whole forest of logs in one load and break up logjams on rivers with a swish of his tail. Legends say that Paul Bunyan scooped out the Great Lakes to provide drinking water for Babe. And when the ox needed new shoes, the blacksmith needed so much iron that a new mine had to be opened in northern Minnesota.

The legend continues in Minnesota for people who visit the Paul Bunyan Center in Brainerd and the huge statues of Paul Bunyan and Babe in Bemidji.

The Kensington Runestone

In 1898 a Swedish immigrant farmer named Olaf Ohman and his son found a huge stone buried on their farm in central Minnesota. A message was carved on the stone in mysterious markings, called runes.

Language experts came to Minnesota to study the stone. Some of the experts said that the message told of Vikings who came from Sweden and Norway to explore the area in 1362.

Some people thought the rock was fake because the wording was not typical of the language in the 1300s. But if the story is true, the stone would prove that Vikings explored Minnesota 130 years before Columbus came to America.

Located near the site where the stone was found, the city of Alexandria, Minnesota, now displays the Kensington Runestone. Alexandria claims to be the Birthplace of America.

Students at this Minneapolis grade school in the 1940s probably learned only a small part of what Indian life was like. Since that time, Minnesota schools have been trying to learn more about the rich culture of the American Indian peoples.

The outbreak of World War I in 1914 brought a demand for Minnesota's products. Wheat was sent overseas to feed soldiers, and iron ore was needed to make guns. During and after the war, the state prospered. But in the 1930s, during the Great Depression, farm prices fell and factory work slowed. Nearly 70 percent of the state's miners lost their jobs.

World War II (1939–1945) again brought a demand for Minnesota's wheat and iron ore. In the 1950s, however, Minnesota's iron ore began to run out. During the next 30 years, mining jobs in the state dropped to almost none.

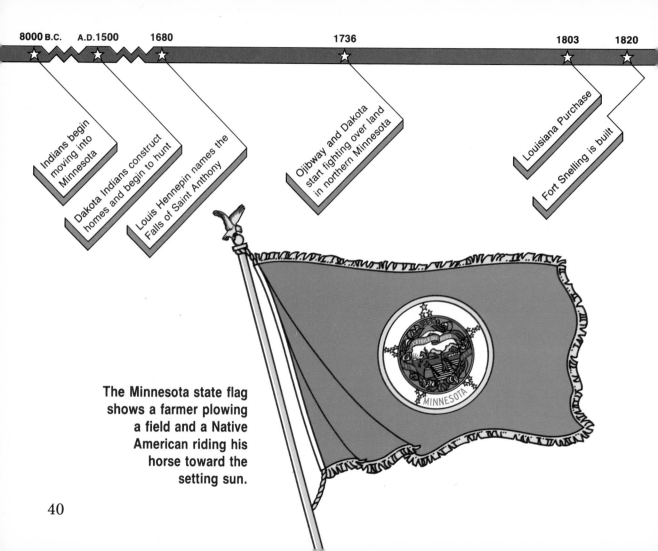

8000 B.C.   A.D.1500   1680   1736   1803   1820

Indians begin moving into Minnesota

Dakota Indians construct homes and begin to hunt

Louis Hennepin names the Falls of Saint Anthony

Ojibway and Dakota start fighting over land in northern Minnesota

Louisiana Purchase

Fort Snelling is built

The Minnesota state flag shows a farmer plowing a field and a Native American riding his horse toward the setting sun.

1858 1862 1873 ⭐⭐ ⭐ Minnesota becomes the 32nd state

U.S.-Dakota Conflict

Grasshoppers destroy crops in southwestern Minnesota

1929 ⭐ Great Depression begins and farm prices fall

1989 ⭐ Community recycling programs begin throughout Minnesota

Gradually, new industries such as trucking, chemicals, electronics, computers, and health care sprang up. More and more farmers began using tractors, which could replace several farmhands. Many of these workers moved to Minnesota's cities.

In the 1970s and 1980s, Minnesotans began to look at their past and at their environment. Many old buildings were restored, and social programs were created to aid Native Americans. People began working to clean up rivers and recycle waste. Although few people still work on Minnesota's farms, the state's farming roots have made Minnesotans hard workers.

41

Speedboats zip down the Mississippi River during the Aquatennial festival boat races in Minneapolis.

Living and Working in Minnesota

The Dakota Indians called their land *minne sota*, which means "land of sky-tinted waters." Minnesota has so many glistening lakes that it is often called the Land of 10,000 Lakes. This natural beauty is part of what makes Minnesota a great place to live or visit.

Most Minnesotans have ancestors from northern Europe. The state also has several other ethnic groups. They include African Americans, Hispanics, and Asians.

Hockey is a favorite sport for many young Minnesotans.

43

Native Americans, though few in number, are found mainly in Minnesota's cities or on the state's 11 reservations. The city of Minneapolis has one of the largest Indian populations of any city in the United States.

Most of the state's 4.4 million people live in cities and towns, many of which are next to water.

About half of all Minnesotans live in the Twin Cities. Minneapolis *(opposite page)* is a growing city with a changing skyline. Saint Paul features the state capitol building *(right).*

Minneapolis and Saint Paul, also called the Twin Cities, straddle the Mississippi River. Minneapolis is the state's largest city, followed by Saint Paul, the state capital. Rochester, Saint Cloud, and Duluth are smaller cities. The busiest port on the Great Lakes, Duluth hugs the southwestern tip of Lake Superior.

Actors from the Children's Theatre Company perform *Cinderella*.

The Twin Cities boast many cultural attractions. The Minneapolis Institute of Arts is Minnesota's largest art museum. The Walker Art Center, a museum of modern art, has an outdoor sculpture garden.

About 60 theaters thrive in the Twin Cities. The Guthrie Theater in Minneapolis has gained a national reputation for its fine plays. The Children's Theatre Company, also in Minneapolis, gives some of the state's youngest talent a chance to act on a professional stage.

The Ordway Music Theatre in Saint Paul was designed to meet the needs of a wide range of performing artists. The Saint Paul

Chamber Orchestra, the Minnesota Opera, the Minnesota Orchestra, and many other groups appear at the Ordway.

Another Saint Paul attraction is the Science Museum of Minnesota, where displays explain the wonders of science and technology. In Duluth, the Canal Park Marine Museum explores the history of commercial fishing in northern Minnesota. The Lake Superior Museum of Transportation features old railroad equipment.

A carriage sculpted from ice is displayed at the Saint Paul Winter Carnival, the largest winter celebration in the nation.

Spectator sports are popular in Minnesota. The Minnesota Twins baseball team and the Minnesota Vikings football team play in the Hubert H. Humphrey Metrodome in Minneapolis. The Minnesota Timberwolves shoot baskets at Minneapolis's Target Center. A

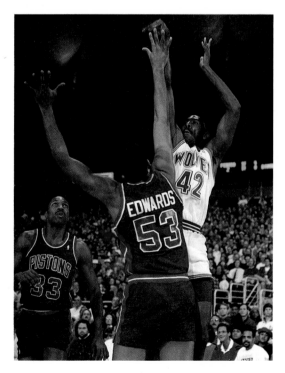

Minnesota sports fans cheer on the Timberwolves *(below)*, the Gophers *(left)*, and the horses racing at Canterbury Downs *(opposite page)*.

popular minor-league baseball team, the St. Paul Saints, plays at Midway Stadium in St. Paul.

The University of Minnesota's teams, all called Gophers, add to the state's sports action. The University of Minnesota, with more than 80,000 students, is one of the largest universities in the nation.

For 60 years, Split Rock Lighthouse guided ships away from Lake Superior's rocky shores. Now part of a state park, the lighthouse features exhibits about the lake's history.

Two young Minnesotans show off their catch.

For many Minnesotans, summer means going to the lake. Minnesota's lakes and rivers lure people to the water to swim, canoe, sail, and water-ski. Long winters encourage skiing, ice-skating, sledding, and ice fishing. Minnesota has 65 state parks and 56 state forests for outdoor recreation.

Though no longer Minnesota's main industries, farming and mining are still important to the state. But both industries have changed greatly. Farmers and miners now use computers and other modern equipment such as trucks, tractors, conveyor belts, and bulldozers to do the work with fewer people.

51

Minnesota's farmers harvest
wheat *(below)* and apples *(right)*.

Only about 5 percent of Minnesota's population lives on farms. Still, the state's farmers produce much of the milk, butter, eggs, turkeys, grains, and some of the vegetables that Americans buy. Major crops include corn, soybeans, hay, beans, and peas. Minnesota's livestock supply dairy products, eggs, and meat. Apples grow well in southern Minnesota.

Mining continues in Minnesota but with fewer jobs than it had during the 1940s. Minnesota supplies 70 percent of the iron ore mined in the nation. Manufacturing employs nearly 18 percent of Minnesota's workers. Computers, medical products, Scotch tape, and flour are a few of the many products made in the state.

Forests in northern Minnesota supply lumber needed for buildings and furniture.

A street vendor sells flowers in downtown Minneapolis. Many service workers in Minnesota have jobs in the state's large cities.

Service jobs, most of which have developed since World War II, create about 73 percent of Minnesota's income and employ most of the state's workers. People in service jobs help other people or businesses. Teachers, store clerks, and bankers are just some of the people who hold service jobs.

Another service industry is medicine. Each year, the Mayo Clinic in Rochester treats thousands of patients. The world-famous clinic has more than 900 doctors.

Minnesota earned one of its first nicknames, the Bread and Butter State, back in the 1800s when grains, flour milling, and dairy products helped the state grow. Minnesota is still growing, and its strength in modern businesses such as computers and health care promises a bright future for the state.

At sand-sculpture contests, Minnesotans show off their creative talents.

Protecting the Environment

Farming has long been one of Minnesota's most widespread industries. More than half of the state's rich soil is used for farming. Because so much of Minnesota's land is devoted to agriculture, farmers affect the quality of water, soil, and crops in the state.

Farmers use fertilizers and pesticides to improve crops by enriching the soil and by killing bugs and weeds. But fertilizers and pesticides can also poison people and animals.

At one time, people did not know the dangers of these chemical mixtures. When huge swarms of grasshoppers covered the state's fields in the 1930s, farmers wanted a quick and sure way to save their crops. One method was to kill the grasshoppers with arsenic—a deadly poison.

Government officials sweetened sawdust or wheat bran with molasses. Then they added arsenic. The mixture was spread across a field as bait. Any grasshopper that ate it died.

In the 1930s, local officials passed out 100-pound (45-kg) sacks of the arsenic mixture to farmers who wanted it. But sometimes farmers didn't actually get their supply until after the grasshoppers were gone.

When the farmers asked the government to take the poison back, they were told to keep it until the grasshoppers returned. People stored the bags of arsenic in various ways. Some put them in a cellar or attic. Some buried them.

Grasshopper

Decades later, mysterious cases of arsenic poisoning cropped up in Minnesota. In 1972, construction workers in Otter Tail County drilled a well and hooked it up to their water supply. Eleven people suffered arsenic poisoning from contaminated water. Some of the victims had permanent damage to their health.

A few years later, five cows in Clay County got into a pile of scrap iron and an old wooden keg that contained arsenic. The cows died. In 1980, twelve more cows died after eating arsenic from an old shed near Two Harbors.

Buried bags of arsenic are a threat to farm animals as well as to people.

When the Minnesota Pollution Control Agency (MPCA) looked into the first case, it discovered the connection between the grasshoppers, the arsenic, and the poisoned water. By the mid-1980s, the MPCA had discovered many more sites where bags of poison had been buried or otherwise stored.

59

The MPCA has offered to remove arsenic from old storage places.

The agency sent out announcements asking people for any information about the grasshopper poison. Hundreds of people called in saying they knew where their family had put the arsenic. The MPCA eventually found a total of 280 storage sites. By 1990 about 50,000 pounds (22,700 kg) of arsenic and sweetened bait had been recovered and shipped to a secure landfill in Oklahoma for safe storage.

The MPCA isn't sure but believes it has found only about one-fourth of the leftover arsenic. Some of the people who might remember where the poison was stored back in the 1930s are no longer living.

As the years pass, the chances of finding the remaining sacks grow slimmer.

The more people learn about how to avoid creating environmental hazards, the less future generations will have to clean up after them. In the 1990s, many people are aware of the need to preserve and conserve resources for the future.

An MPCA worker digs through frozen ground to remove bags of arsenic that were buried years ago.

Minnesota's Famous People

CHARLES
LINDBERGH

Charles Lindbergh (1902–1974) grew up in Little Falls, Minnesota. In 1927 he became the first person to fly solo across the Atlantic Ocean. His book about the flight, titled *The Spirit of St. Louis,* won a Pulitzer Prize in 1954.

Jeanette Piccard (1895–1981) was born in Chicago but lived in Minneapolis much of her life. In 1934 she became the first woman to pilot a hot-air balloon to the stratosphere, an upper layer of the earth's atmosphere.

Will Steger (born 1945) became famous in 1986 when he made a trek with dog sleds to the North Pole. In 1990 he participated in the first trip across Antarctica's greatest width—3,741 miles (6,023 km). With his team, he journeyed across the frozen Arctic Ocean from Russia to Canada in 1995.

JEANETTE ▶
PICCARD

WILL ▶
STEGER

BUSINESS & FINANCIAL LEADERS

The Cargill family owns Cargill, Inc., the largest privately held company in the United States. Cargill, Inc., began in 1865 as a grain trading company. Its headquarters are in Minnetonka, Minnesota.

Curt Carlson (born 1914) started Carlson Companies in 1938. The company, which is based in Minnesota, deals with financial investments, marketing, and real estate.

George Draper Dayton (1857–1938) moved to Minnesota from New York in 1883. In 1902 he founded The Dayton Company in Minneapolis. The Dayton Hudson Corporation, based in Minnesota, now owns one of the largest department-store chains in the United States.

William McKnight (1887–1978) took a job in 1907 with 3M's sandpaper factory in Duluth, Minnesota. Just nine years later, he became president of 3M, and for the next fifty years he led the company to become an international giant.

◄ GEORGE DAYTON

BOB DYLAN ▶

◄ JUDY GARLAND

ENTERTAINERS & ARTISTS

Bob Dylan (born 1941) grew up in Hibbing, Minnesota. Dylan, a songwriter and singer known especially for his protest lyrics, influenced folk and rock music during the 1960s and 1970s.

Judy Garland (1922–1969), a singer and actress, is famous for her roll as Dorothy in *The Wizard of Oz*. She also starred in the movie musicals *Meet Me in St. Louis* and *Easter Parade*. Garland was born in Grand Rapids, Minnesota.

▲ ☥

(Prince Roger Nelson) (born 1958) grew up in Minneapolis. A pop singer, songwriter, and musician, he has made albums and several films, including *Purple Rain*. Formerly known as Prince, he has his own record company, Paisley Park.

Charles Schulz (born 1922) has been drawing the "Peanuts" comic strip since 1950. "Peanuts" is found in more than 2,000 newspapers around the world. Schulz was born in Minneapolis.

◄ CHARLES SCHULZ

63

MEDICAL INNOVATORS

Elizabeth Kenny (1880–1952) moved from Australia to Minnesota in 1940. A nurse, Kenny developed a method to treat victims of poliomyelitis, a virus that weakens muscles and sometimes even causes them to stop working. Kenny's work pioneered the field of physical therapy.

Charles Horace Mayo (1865–1939) and **William James Mayo** (1861–1939) helped establish a medical center that grew to be the widely famed Mayo Clinic in Rochester, Minnesota. The brothers also cofounded the Mayo Foundation for Medical Education and Research.

CHARLES ► MAYO

▲ ELIZABETH KENNY

WILLIAM MAYO ►

◄ HUBERT HUMPHREY

WALTER ► MONDALE

POLITICIANS

Hubert H. Humphrey (1911–1978) served as a U.S. senator from Minnesota for 23 years. While in the Senate, he introduced a bill to establish the Peace Corps, and he fought for passage of the 1964 Civil Rights Act. Humphrey was vice president of the United States from 1965 to 1969 and ran unsuccessfully for president in 1968.

Walter Mondale (born 1928), a native of Elmore, Minnesota, served as a U.S. senator for 12 years. He was vice president of the United States from 1977 to 1981. In 1984 Mondale ran for president but did not win the election.

Harold Stassen (born 1907) was elected governor of Minnesota in 1938 at the age of 31, making him the youngest governor of any state in the history of the United States. In 1945 Stassen helped found the United Nations. He has been a frequent but unsuccessful candidate for national political office.

Halsey Hall (1898-1977) covered Minnesota sports for more than 50 years as a broadcaster and newspaper columnist. During a baseball broadcast in 1934, he became the first announcer to use the expression "Holy Cow!" The phrase became his trademark. Hall grew up in Saint Paul.

Jill Trenary (born 1969) grew up in Minnetonka. A figure skater, Trenary won the ladies competition at the 1990 World Figure Skating Championships. She was the U.S. Ladies Champion in 1987 and 1989 and also skated in the 1988 Olympic Games.

◀ HALSEY HALL

F. SCOTT FITZGERALD ▶

▲ SINCLAIR LEWIS

GARRISON KEILLOR ▶

WRITERS

F. Scott Fitzgerald (1896-1940), born in Saint Paul, is famous for his novels that are set in the 1920s. His books include *This Side of Paradise* and *The Great Gatsby*.

Wanda Gág (1893-1946), from New Ulm, Minnesota, learned the art of storytelling from her family. A master at weaving together stories and drawings, Gág won awards for her children's books—including *Millions of Cats*.

Garrison Keillor (born 1942) became widely known for his stories about Lake Wobegon on the radio program "A Prairie Home Companion." A native of Anoka, Minnesota, Keillor writes humorous books and magazine articles.

Sinclair Lewis (1885-1951) was the first American to be awarded the Nobel Prize for literature. He used his hometown, Sauk Centre, Minnesota, as a model for his most famous book, *Main Street*.

Facts-at-a-Glance

Nickname: Gopher State
Song: "Hail! Minnesota"
Motto: *L'Etoile du Nord* (The Star of the North)
Flower: pink and white lady's-slipper
Tree: Norway pine
Bird: common loon

Population: 4,375,099*
Rank in population, nationwide: 20th
Area: 84,402 sq mi (218,601 sq km)
Rank in area, nationwide: 12th
Date and ranking of statehood:
    May 11, 1858, the 32nd state
Capital: Saint Paul
Major cities (and populations*):
    Minneapolis (368,383), Saint Paul (272,235),
    Bloomington (86,335), Duluth (85,493),
    Rochester (70,745)
U.S. senators: 2
U.S. representatives: 8
Electoral votes: 10

Places to visit: Fort Snelling near Minneapolis,
Ironworld near Chisholm, Murphy's Landing near
Shakopee, Minnesota Zoo in Apple Valley, Science
Museum of Minnesota in Saint Paul

*1990 census

Annual events: St. Paul Winter Carnival (Jan.),
John Beargrease Sled Dog Race near Duluth (Jan.),
Ice Box Days in International Falls (Jan.), Swayed
Pines Folk Fest in Collegeville (April), Aquatennial
festival in Minneapolis (July), Fisherman's Picnic in
Grand Marais (July), Renaissance Festival in Shak-
opee (Sept.), Oktoberfest in New Ulm (Oct.)

66

Natural resources: fertile soil, forests, lakes and rivers, taconite, iron ore, granite, peat, limestone, sandstone, sand and gravel

Agricultural products: milk, hogs, turkeys, soybeans, corn, hay, wheat, barley, potatoes, sugar beets, rye, apples, green peas, carrots, onions

Manufactured goods: machinery, flour, metal products, chemicals, printed materials, paper products, medical products, computers and computer equipment

ENDANGERED AND THREATENED SPECIES
Mammals—gray wolf
Birds—Sprague's pipit, Baird's sparrow, burrowing owl, chestnut-collared longspur, piping plover, peregrine falcon
Reptiles—five-lined skink, wood turtle, Blanding's turtle
Freshwater mollusks—Higgin's eye, fat pocketbook
Plants—kitten-tails, wolf's spike rush, Indian ricegrass, knotty pearlwort, nodding saxifrage, bog adder's mouth, Norwegian draba, rams-head lady's-slipper

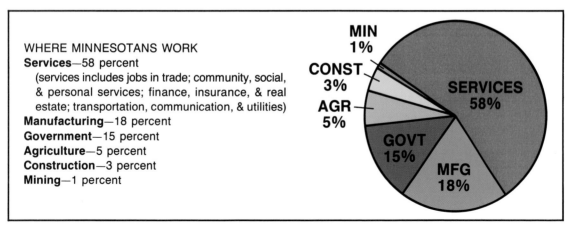

WHERE MINNESOTANS WORK
Services—58 percent
    (services includes jobs in trade; community, social, & personal services; finance, insurance, & real estate; transportation, communication, & utilities)
Manufacturing—18 percent
Government—15 percent
Agriculture—5 percent
Construction—3 percent
Mining—1 percent

MIN 1%
CONST 3%
AGR 5%
SERVICES 58%
GOVT 15%
MFG 18%

Chippewa (CHIP-uh-waw)

Chouart des Groselliers,
Médard (shwar day groh-zeh-YAY,
MAY-dahr)

Duluth (duh-LOOTH)

Hennepin, Louis (HEHN-uh-pihn,
LOO-ihs)

Iroquis (IHR-uh-kwoy)

Itasca (eye-TAS-kuh)

Minneapolis (mihn-ee-AP-uh-luhs)

Ojibway (oh-JIHB-way)

Radisson, Pierre Esprit (RA-dih-suhn,
pee-AYR ehs-PREE)

Saint Croix (saynt KROY)

Sioux (SOO)

Glossary

bluff A steep, high bank, found especially along a river; a cliff.

drift A mixture of clay, sand, gravel, and boulders deposited by a glacier, plus any materials added to this mixture by the running water of a melting glacier. Areas where drift has been deposited have very good soil for farming.

glacier A large body of ice and snow that moves slowly over land.

Great Lakes A chain of five lakes in Canada and the northern United States. They are Lakes Superior, Michigan, Huron, Erie, and Ontario.

ice age A period when ice sheets cover large regions of the earth. The term *Ice Age* usually refers to the most recent one, called the Pleistocene, which began almost 2 million years ago.

immigrant A person who moves to a foreign country and settles there.

missionary A person sent out by a religious group to spread its beliefs to other people.

prairie A large area of level or gently rolling grassy land with few trees.

reservation Public land set aside by the government to be used by Native Americans.

treaty An agreement between two or more groups, usually having to do with peace or trade.

wetland A swamp, marsh, or other low, wet area that often borders a river, lake, or ocean. Wetlands support many different kinds of plants and animals.

Index

Agriculture, 16, 25, 32, 33–35, 39, 41, 51, 52, 53, 54–55, 56–57, 58–59
Animals, 16–17, 19, 20, 22, 26, 27
Arsenic, 58–61
Arts, 46–47

Bluffs, 12–13
Boundary Waters, 11
Bunyan, Paul, 37

Canada, 9, 11
Cities, 6, 7, 13, 21, 24, 27, 44–45, 48–49, 54, 59. *See also* Duluth; Minneapolis; Saint Paul
Civil War, 29, 32
Climate, 6, 8, 14–15, 19, 20, 50

Dakota Conflict, 30–31
Driftless Area, 11, 12–13
Drift Plains, 11, 12
Duluth, 36, 45, 47

Economy, 39, 51, 53–55
Education, 26, 49
Environment, 41, 57–61

Ethnic makeup, 26–27, 29, 33, 43–44
Explorers, 20–21

Falls of Saint Anthony, 21, 25
Fish and fishing, 7, 17, 47, 51
Flag, 40
Flour mills, 25, 37
Food processing, 41, 53
Forests and forestry, 15, 20, 25, 27, 51, 53, 57
Fort Snelling, 25, 26, 32
France, 20, 21, 22, 24
Fur trading, 21, 22, 23, 24, 27

Glaciers, 9, 11, 12, 13, 19
Grasshoppers, 34–35, 58, 60
Great Lakes, 9, 22, 36, 45

Hennepin, Louis, 21
History, 18–41; ancient, 9, 19–20; exploration and traders, 16, 20–24; 1800s, 24–29, 30–31, 32–36, 38, 58; 1900s, 6, 39–41, 58; settlers, 25–27, 29, 30–31, 33–35; statehood, 29; timeline, 40–41
Homestead Act, 33

Hunting, 19, 20, 22

Indians, 18, 19–22, 24, 25–27, 29, 30–31, 33, 40, 44; Dakota (Sioux), 20–21, 22, 24–26, 28–29, 30–31, 33; Iroquois, 22; Ojibway (Chippewa), 22, 24, 26, 29
Iron ore, 36, 39, 53

Jobs, 33, 39, 41, 51, 53–55

Kensington Runestone, 38

Lakes, 6, 7, 9, 11, 13, 17, 18, 20, 36, 43, 45, 50, 51, 57. *See also* Great Lakes; Superior, Lake
Louisiana Purchase, 24
Lumbering, 25, 27, 32, 36, 53, 57

Manufacturing, 39, 41, 53
Mayo Clinic, 54
Military, 25, 29, 32, 39
Mining, 36, 39, 51, 53
Minneapolis, 21, 37, 44–45, 46, 48–49, 54, 59

Minnesota: boundaries and location, 9, 10, 11; ethnic makeup, 26–27, 29, 33, 43–44; flag of, 40; Facts-at-a-Glance, 66–67; Famous People, 62–65; maps and charts, 10; nicknames, 9, 32–33, 43, 54; origin of name, 43; population, 29, 44–45; statehood, 29
Minnesota Pollution Control Agency (MPCA), 59–61
Minnesota River, 13, 25, 29
Minnesota Territory, 27, 29
Mississippi River, 13, 21, 25, 26, 27, 42, 45
Museums, 47

Native Americans. *See* Indians

Pike, Zebulon, 25
Plants, 15, 16–17
Pollution, 57–61
Population, 29, 44–45

Railroads, 32–33, 35, 36, 47
Recycling, 41, 57
Rivers, 13, 21, 23, 25, 26, 27, 29, 41, 45. *See also* Minnesota River; Mississippi River; Saint Croix River

Saint Croix River, 13, 27
Saint Paul, 6, 27, 36, 45, 46–47
Slavery, 29, 32
Sports and recreation, 6, 7, 14, 41, 43, 48–49, 50–51, 55
Superior, Lake, 9, 11, 20, 36, 45, 51
Superior Upland, 11, 12

Transportation, 23, 27, 32, 35, 36, 41

Treaties, 28, 29, 30–31
Twin Cities, 45, 46. *See also* Minneapolis; Saint Paul

United States government, 24, 25, 26, 28, 29, 33, 58–59, 60

Wars and battles, 24, 29, 30–31, 32, 38. *See also* Civil War
Waterskiing, 6, 51

Acknowledgments:

Maryland Cartographics, Inc., pp. 2, 10; Emily Slowinski, pp. 2-3, 8, 19; Jack Lindstrom, p. 6; Rollerblade Inc., p. 7; Louise K. Broman / Root Resources, p. 9; Kay Shaw, pp. 11, 12, 26, 47, 56-57, 62 (bottom), 71; Jim Simondet, pp. 13, 51; Lucille Sukalo, pp. 14 (left), 15, 43, 52 (right), 53, 59, 69; Richard Thom / Visuals Unlimited, p. 14 (right); Lynn M. Stone, pp. 16, 17; John Polis, p. 18; National Archives of Canada, Ottawa, pp. 20 (C-114467 – detail), 23 (C-13456); Minnesota Historical Society, pp. 21, 27, 28, 31 (bottom), 32, 33, 35, 36, 64 (bottom left); Len Rue, Jr. / Visuals Unlimited, p. 22; Northwest Magazine, Minnesota Historical Society, p. 24; Library of Congress, p. 25; Minneapolis Public Library and Information Center, pp. 30, 34; Smithsonian Institution, pp. 31 (top) (photo no. 3505-B), 62 (top left); Minnesota Office of Tourism, pp. 37, 44; Viking Research, Bill Holman, Alexandria, Minnesota, p. 38; Independent Picture Service, pp. 39, 64 (bottom right); G. Paul Herda, pp. 42, 55; Karen Sirvaitis, pp. 45, 54; The Greater Minneapolis Convention & Visitors Association, pp. 46, 48, 49 (left); Minnesota Timberwolves, p. 49 (right); James Blank / Root Resources, p. 50; Harvest States Cooperatives, St. Paul, Minnesota, p. 52 (left); Gerry Lemmo, p. 58; Minnesota Water and Pollution Control Agency, pp. 60, 61; Dearborn Historical Museum, p. 62 (top right); Dayton Hudson Corporation, p. 63 (top left); John Rott, News–Tribune & Herald, Duluth, Minnesota, p. 63 (right); Hollywood Book & Poster Co., p. 63 (center left & center right); Roddy McDowall, p. 63 (bottom); Minneapolis Times Newspaper file, Minneapolis Public Library, p. 64 (top left); Mayo Foundation Historical Collection, p. 64 (top middle, top right); Marty Nordstrom, Minnesota Historical Society, p. 64 (bottom left); WCCO Radio, p. 65 (top); Charles Scribner's Sons, p. 65 (bottom center); Sinclair Lewis Foundation, Inc., p. 65 (bottom left); Will Crockett, Minnesota Public Radio, p. 65 (bottom right); Jean Matheny, p. 66.